GIANTS
IN THE LAND
THE COMING NEPHILIM

REONA MARTIN

Giants In The Land: The Coming Nephilim
Published by Reona Martin Ministries
USA

For book-ordering please visit the website:
www.reonamartinministries.com

All Scripture quotations unmarked are taken from The New American Standard Bible, The Ryrie Study Bible, copyright 1995 by the Moody Bible Institute, Chicago, Illinois. Used by Permission.

Scripture Quotations Marked NKJV The New King James Version, Copyright 1979, 1980, 1982 By Thomas Nelson, Inc., Publishers, Nashville, Tennessee. Used By Permission.

Scripture quotations marked KJV are taken from the King James Bible.

Scripture quotations marked Septuagint are taken from the Septuagint With Apocrypha: Greek And English As Translated By Lancelot C. L. Brenton, Hendrickson Publishers; Peabody, Massachusetts, reprint of the April 1, 1986 edition.

Copyright © 2015 By Reona Martin
All Rights Reserved.

Revised Edition 2021

Martin, Reona
Giants In The Land: The Coming Nephilim

ISBN   978-0-9708936-1-1

Edited by: Judith Howard Ellis

Contents and/or cover design may not be reproduced in whole or in part in any form, stored in a retrieval system, or transmitted in any form without the express written consent of the author.

GIANTS IN THE LAND: THE COMING NEPHILIM

REONA MARTIN

REONA MARTIN MINISTRIES

E-mail: reona@reonamartinministries.com

Website: www.reonamartinministries.com

CONTENTS

Special Thanks

Forward

Introduction

CHAPTER 1
    Where Do Giants Come From?   13

CHAPTER 2
    Types Of Giants   19

CHAPTER 3
    Coming Giants   29

CHAPTER 4
    Generations Of Giant Descendants Are Coming   37

CHAPTER 5
    Giant Infiltration   49

CHAPTER 6
What Will Giant Pollution Look Like?   55

CHAPTER 7
Giants Are Not Redeemed   63

CHAPTER 8
God Wants To Preserve Life   67

CHAPTER 9
Activities Of Future Giants   71

CHAPTER 10
What Can We Expect?   79

Glossary   83

Endnotes   87

SPECIAL THANKS

I would like to thank my family: my father, Gilbert, my mother Jean, my sister Beverly and my brother Joseph for their loving support throughout the writing of this book. I also would like to thank Judy Howard Ellis whose behind-the-scenes help was a tremendous blessing.

FORWARD

You may have read many Internet discussions about giants or seen TV shows about fallen angels, but what I want to offer you is a Bible-based study on this subject. Mainly, I want to do so because the Bible says we will see these strange beings again.

In my book, "Giants In The Land: The Coming Nephilim," I provide a solid biblical foundation supporting the fact that real, physical giants will reappear on earth in the near future. This fact clearly emerges when connecting Old and New Testament Scriptures to gain a comprehensive biblical perspective.

The intent of this book is to examine the presence of giants in ancient history and address the global impact of giants and their descendants during the end times.

INTRODUCTION

Giants existed during early civilization. According to Genesis, giants originated from unauthorized unions between rebellious angels and daughters of men. Intimidating and violent, giants terrorized God's people and opposed His ways and plans for humans and earth.

Like many Bible students, I used to think ancient giants symbolized obstacles that blocked my way in life. My biggest takeaway from that limited biblical understanding was that God would help me overcome challenges such as sickness, money problems, and unemployment. True. Giants *do* represent spiritual obstacles that oppose the work of God's kingdom and the activities of His saints. But giants aren't merely metaphorical. Giants existed as physical beings in ancient times, and one day they will reappear as physical beings. They will participate in Satan's wicked plan to subvert the will of God for men and women.

Giants, as I will explain in this book, will play a major role in an end time battle.

CHAPTER 1
WHERE DO GIANTS COME FROM?

Long before Hollywood writers penned scripts about invading extraterrestrials, the Bible described a hybrid race who tried to dominate the ancient world. The Scriptures record their origins and appearance. In Genesis 6, the Bible offers clues about this hybrid race in a passage that reads like a movie with an incredible plot:

> Now it came about, when men began to multiply on the face of the land, and daughters were born

to them, that the sons of God saw that the daughters of men were beautiful; and they took wives for themselves, whomever they chose. Then the LORD said, "My Spirit shall not strive with man forever, because he also is flesh; nevertheless his days shall be one hundred and twenty years." The Nephilim were on the earth in those days, and also afterward, when the sons of God came in to the daughters of men, and they bore *children* to them. Those were the mighty men who *were* of old, men of renown. (Genesis 6:1-4)

This passage doesn't borrow a few lines from a comic book. Ancient giants existed, and the Bible says so. Three groups named in Genesis 6 can help us understand the origin of giants:

Sons of God: The Old Testament uses the phrase "sons of God" only a few times (Genesis 6:2 and 6:4, Job 1:6, 2:1 and 38:7). Let's look at one of these passages. Take Job 1:6: "Now there was a day when the sons of God came to present themselves before the LORD, and Satan also came among them." The verse implies that

Satan was among the "sons of God." This helps us see that the sons of God refer to angels in the Old Testament. However, sons of God in the New Testament refer to believers in God who accept Jesus Christ as their Savior and Lord (Luke 20:36).

Daughters of Men: The Hebrew word for men in the phrase is *'adam*.[1] Therefore, the "daughters of men" were daughters of Adamites. They weren't the daughters of angels. These women descended from Adam and Eve. In other words, they were human beings like you and me.

Nephilim: These Nephilim were the offspring of angels who had relations with Adamite women. Nephilim goes back to the Hebrew word *Naphal* which means to fall.[2] Not all scholars agree that this is the meaning of the word. The Septuagint, a Greek translation of the Hebrew Scriptures, renders the word Nephilim as *gigantes*. When some translators translated it into English, they used the word giants.

Genesis 6:4 refers to the Nephilim as "mighty men." The Hebrew term for "mighty men" is *gibborim*, which means strong ones.[3] The Septuagint chose to translate both terms Nephilim and *gibborim* as giants in this passage.

To sum it up, the Bible classifies angels who had relations with human women as sons of God and identifies giants as the offspring of these unsanctified unions.

About those rebellious angels

Angels have a free will to choose right from wrong. Satan chose to rebel against God along with some other angels (Luke 10:18 and Revelation 12). Angels can choose to serve God or rebel against Him. In the case of those angels who had relations with human women, they chose to rebel against God.

Can angels rebel today in the same way they did in Genesis 6? Yes, they can. Let's look at the verse again. "The Nephilim were on the earth in those days, and also afterward, when the sons of God came into the daughters of men, and they bore *children* to them. Those were the mighty men who *were* of old, men of renown" (Genesis 6:4). The phrase "also afterward" is what I want to point out to you. A stopping point isn't mentioned in the Genesis 6:4 passage, and it doesn't say that this awful activity won't reoccur in the future. In other words, the Bible doesn't say that a similar rebellion won't happen again!

GIANTS IN THE LAND

CHAPTER 2
TYPES OF GIANTS

Forbidden unions between rebellious angels and human women produced races of giants that were unlike normal humans. They were extremely tall, remarkably strong, and violent. Even their descendants were of great height and strength.

Nephilim

The Bible mentions that the Nephilim lived on the earth during the time of Moses, and before. When the twelve Israelite spies surveyed Canaan, they delivered a report riddled with fear. "There also we saw the Nephilim (the sons of Anak are part of the Nephilim); and we became like grasshoppers in our sight, and so we were in their sight" (Numbers 13:33).

Two of the spies gave a fearless view of Canaan. Joshua and Caleb spoke in faith because they knew God surpassed the tallest and most intimidating giant. After Moses had died, Joshua led the Israelites in battles that destroyed many of the descendants of the giants.

In addition to the Nephilim, the Bible mentions these giant tribes: the Rephaim, Anakim, Emim, Zamzummin and Avvim. Deuteronomy 2 identifies the various giant tribes. Here are brief descriptions of each group.

Rephaim

The Rephaim were a giant tribe during early Biblical times. It's not easily observed in some Bible translations that the Rephaim were giants. The Septuagint does refer to them as giants. Let's look at two passages from the Septuagint. "For only Og the king of Basan was left of the Raphain *[Rephaim]*." (Deuteronomy 3:11) Here is the next passage. "And Og king of Basan, who dwelt in Astaroth and in Edrain, was left of the giants." (Joshua 12:4) From the Septuagint rendering we can observe that the Rephaim were giants.

GIANTS IN THE LAND

The Rephaim lived east of the Jordan in Bashan. The Valley of Rephaim, located southwest of Jerusalem, bears their name. Today the valley is called el-Bukei′a.[1]

Og was one of the last Rephaim. He ruled over the Bashan area, a region known today as the Golan Heights. Og reigned during the time of Moses.

> For only Og the king of Basan was left of the Raphain: behold, his bed *was* a bed of iron; behold, *it is* in the chief city of the children of Ammon; the length of it *is* nine cubits, and the breadth of it four cubits, according to the cubit of a man. (Deuteronomy 3:11 Septuagint)

Given the cubic is approximately 21 inches, Og's bed was about 15 3/4 feet long and 7 feet wide.[2] Some scholars believe a cubic was 18 inches. Either way, the size of the bed indicates that Og was enormous.

The Bible says Og and his kingdom battled the Israelites as they traveled to Canaan. Og refused to allow the Israelites to pass through their land. But their resistance didn't stop Israel. Moses and the Israelites destroyed Og and his kingdom. The Israelites seized sixty fortified cities, along with many un-walled towns because the Lord God was their help (Deuteronomy 3:1-17).

Anakim

The Anakim were regarded as the Rephaim (Deuteronomy 2:10 and 11). The Anakim giants lived in southern and southwestern Canaan, in the neighborhood of Hebron. Their height and long necks revealed their identity. In fact, the name Anakim means "long-necked ones."[3]

Emim

Emim means "terrors."[4] Like the Anakim, they were regarded as the Rephaim. This population of giants lived in Ar (Genesis 14:5). The exact location of this city is unknown. The children of Lot succeeded them. (Deuteronomy 2:10).

Zamzummin

The name of these giants means "plotters," as in to devise, plan, consider or purpose.[5] The Lord destroyed the Zamzummin before the Ammonites, and they dwelt in their stead (Deuteronomy 2:20 and 21). The Ammonites called the Rephaim, the Zamzummin.

Avvim

The Avvim who were giants were also called the Avvites. Avvim means "ruins."[6] They were early occupants of Philistia. Deuteronomy 2:23 says: "And the Avvim, who dwelt in villages as far as Gaza, the Caphtorim who came from Caphtor, destroyed them and lived in their place."

Descendants of giants

The Bible indicates giants produced extremely tall descendants; today we loosely use the term giants to refer to them. However, these descendants were not as tall and imposing as the Rephaim or Anakim. The descendants of giants were merely large, polluted beings.

The Amorites were such beings. Scriptures indicate the Amorites were the offspring of the Rephaim. Deuteronomy 3:1 and 2 and Joshua 2:10 reveal this in an account of the Israelites' journey to Canaan. Let's look at Deuteronomy 3:1 and 2 first. "Then we turned and went up the road to Bashan, and Og, king of Bashan, with all his people came out to meet us in battle at Edrei. But the LORD said to me, 'Do not fear him, for I have delivered him and all his people and his land into your hand; and you shall do to him just as you did to Sihon king of the Amorites, who lived at Heshbon.'" Now let's look at Joshua 2:10 because it reveals who were Og's people. "For we have heard how the LORD dried up the water of the Red Sea before you when you came out of Egypt, and what you did to the two kings of the Amorites who were beyond the Jordan, to Sihon and Og, whom you utterly destroyed." Observe the Amorites were considered Og's people.

The Book of Jubilees, an ancient outside biblical text that is referenced in the Bible, explains, "the former terrible giants, the Rephaim, gave way to the Amorites, an evil and sinful people whose wickedness surpasses that of any other, and whose life will be cut short on earth." (Book of Jubilees xxix. [9] 11)[7]

The Amorites descended from a giant. I'm calling your attention to this to emphasize that although the

Amorites were not "giants" they were very tall and exceedingly strong. Amos 2:9 and 10 states:

> Yet it was I who destroyed the Amorite before them, though his height was like the height of the cedars and he was strong as the oaks; I even destroyed his fruit above and his root below. It was I who brought you up from the land of Egypt, and I led you in the wilderness forty years, that you might take possession of the land of the Amorite.

Who was Goliath?

Many of us know the Bible story of how the young Israelite David fought Goliath because the Philistine warrior taunted the armies of the living God. David stood before this tall being and brought him down with a stone flung from his sling. Then David beheaded Goliath with the warrior's own sword.

Who was Goliath? 1 Chronicles 20:8 says that Goliath descended from a giant-polluted line. Some Bible scholars refer to him as a giant because of his height, but the Bible describes him as a "champion" and not a giant. First Samuel 17:4 says: "Then a champion came out from the armies of the Philistines named Goliath, from Gath, whose height was six cubits and a span." Champion is the Hebrew term *'iysh* which means male, husband, champion, great man, or person.[8]

Notice that the term *'adam* is not used to describe this enemy of Israel. The Bible calls Adam both – an Adamite and an *'iysh* – a term used in Genesis 2:23: "The man said, 'This is now bone of my bones, and flesh of my flesh; she shall be called woman, because she was taken out of man.' "

When the Bible refers to Adam in connection with mankind, it uses the word *'adam*."[9] Such is the case with the first word "man" in Genesis 2:23. When the Bible refers to Adam as a husband, *'iysh* is used.[10] This is the case with the second word for "man" in the same verse. Simply put, *'iysh* means a male and *'adam* means mankind.

But tall beings like Goliath who descended from a giant *were not* Adamites.[11] In other words, they weren't human. In the case of Goliath, his height was about 10 1/2 feet tall given that a cubic is 21 inches.

Many descendants of giants are mentioned in the Bible: Jebusites, Amorites, Hittites, Perizzites, Girgashites, Kadmonites, Hivites, Horites, Philistines (some of them), Arvadites, Zemarites, Hamathites, Sinites, Arkites, Kenites and the Kenizzites. There were others besides these according to the Bible (Genesis 10 and 15, Exodus 13:5, Deuteronomy 2, and Joshua 24).

Understanding the types of giants and their descendants will help us recognize similar groups of polluted beings in the days to come.

GIANTS IN THE LAND

CHAPTER 3
COMING GIANTS

Many of us are aware that a distressing time will occur just before Jesus returns – a time when God and the Lord Jesus Christ will pour out wrath upon the earth because of grave wickedness and gross sin. The Bible calls this period the Day of the Lord, and it will occur close to the end of the age. I have often thought about what this time would look like. When I started tracing clues about the giants, I made an unexpected discovery. Isaiah prophesies that giants will play a role in future events. Yes, you read that correctly. Bible scholars have discussed many end time scenarios extensively. What many scholars have overlooked is that giants also will be present during the end times.

Isaiah's prophecy says:

The burden against Babylon which Isaiah the son of Amos saw. "Lift up a banner on the high mountain, raise your voice to them; wave your hand, that they may enter the gates of the nobles. I have commanded My sanctified ones; I have also called My mighty ones for My anger – those who rejoice in My exaltation." The noise of a multitude in the mountains, like that of many people! A tumultuous noise of the kingdoms of nations gathered together! The LORD of hosts musters the army for battle. They come from a far country, from the end of heaven even the LORD and His weapons of indignation, to destroy the whole land. Wail, for the day of the LORD is at hand! It will come as destruction from the Almighty. (Isaiah 13:1-6 NKJV)

God uses three groups to accomplish the destruction of end-time Babylon. First, He will use His sanctified ones; the Amplified Bible calls them "designated ones." God will set them apart to carry out His judgment. These may not necessarily be righteous people.

He also will use mighty ones according to Isaiah 13:3. Mighty ones in Hebrew is the term *gibborim* which means strong ones.[1] The Septuagint uses the actual word giants in its translation of Isaiah 13:3 and 4. Here is the passage as rendered in the Septuagint: "I give command, and I bring them: giants are coming to fulfil my wrath, rejoicing at the same time and insulting. A voice of many nations on the mountain, *even* like *to that* of many nations;" In this context, the word *gibborim* refers to giants. Observe the language Isaiah uses in the passage. He describes the giants "like" of many nations - not "of" many nations. These giants will participate in the annihilation of Babylon during the end times.

A third group God uses to fight against Babylon are the Medes, known today as Iran. Let me pause here. I didn't present that part of the Isaiah prophecy that mentions the Medes. Here is that part now: "Behold, I am going to stir up the Medes against them, who will not value silver or take pleasure in gold" (Isaiah 13:17).

Where will these future giants come from?

Isaiah writes that these giants will come "from a far country, from the end of heaven" (Isaiah 13:5b NKJV). At first, I thought these giants were coming from the sky and perhaps from another inhabited planet because part of this phrase says they are coming from "the end of heaven." Robert Jamieson, author of the "Commentary Critical and Explanatory on the Whole Bible," says the expression "the end of heaven" means "east."[2]

Babylon

It seems far-fetched that Babylon will once again be a thriving city. Babylon lies mostly in ruins today, but the ancient site still ignites controversy. Will there be a future and literal Babylon? Some believe the prophecy about its destruction already has occurred, and that the city won't return. But when Cyrus the Great assumed control of Babylon in 539 B.C., he didn't destroy it. Alexander the Great defeated the Persians and took over the city in 331 B.C., but he didn't destroy it, either. The ancient city simply fell into decay.

Where will the future Babylon be located?

According to Jeremiah 51:53 and 54, the land of the Chaldeans is the future site of Babylon. The Chaldeans began as an ancient people who were associated with the Babylon area.[3] A large part of the ancient region of the Chaldeans is located at the northwest end of the Persian Gulf. This area is known for the most part as Iraq. End-time Babylon may be rebuilt upon the ancient ruins, or in another spot within the geographical location where the ancient Chaldeans once ruled.

Babylon will possess religious and economic dominance that will influence the nations. The Bible says that the kings of the earth and the financially wealthy will embrace Babylon. Tragically, Babylon will multiply its sins. Babylon will perform violent acts against mankind (Revelation 18).

God will punish Babylon for its violence and sin. "And Babylon, the beauty of kingdoms, the glory of the Chaldeans' pride, will be as when God overthrew

Sodom and Gomorrah. It will never be inhabited or lived in from generation to generation; nor will the Arab pitch *his* tent there, nor will shepherds make *their flocks* lie down there" (Isaiah 13:19 and 20). Babylon will be destroyed by violence, and suddenly, even by fire. Babylon's destruction is part of God's judgment for all the evil it will do (Revelation 17 and 18).

Plans to rebuild Babylon

Babylon was a magnificent city for many centuries. It gained a reputation for its laws, accounting, and astrology. Plans are under way for the city of Babylon to be rebuilt right now. A media note was issued by the U.S. Department of State on January 7, 2009 that reported:

> The U.S. Department of State is pleased to announce its support of a project to develop a plan for the management and preservation of the archaeological site of Babylon. Funded to nearly $700,000, this project will be carried out by the World Monuments Fund (WMF) in partnership with the Iraq State Board of Antiquities and Heritage (SBAH).[4]

Isaiah 13 has a lot to say about Babylon's end. Isaiah prophesied that giants, along with some humans, will attack Babylon. What I've discovered is that not only will giants attack Babylon, but giants will live there.

GIANTS IN THE LAND

CHAPTER 4
GENERATIONS OF GIANT DESCENDANTS ARE COMING

Knowing that giants will appear on earth before the Second Coming of Christ didn't concern me at first. I thought they would appear very close to the end of the age, and that more than likely I wouldn't be around to see them. But after reading Isaiah's entire prophecy, I know that not only will giants attack Babylon, but a giant and several generations of its descendants will inhabit Babylon. This shocking information caused me to reconsider how soon I think giants will appear on earth.

I discovered this eye-opening truth when I studied Isaiah 14:22 and 23. The Scripture says:

> "I will rise up against them," declares the LORD of hosts, "and will cut off from Babylon name and survivors, offspring and posterity," declares the LORD. "I will also make it a possession for the hedgehog and swamps of water, and I will sweep it with the broom of destruction," declares the LORD of hosts.

God will destroy several generations in Babylon. They can be identified by these terms: "the name," "survivors," "offspring" and "posterity." God often embeds information about a topic in plain sight. In this case, Isaiah uses terms that mean more than a string of words to emphasize a point. The first term represents a giant and the other terms signify the giant's descendants.

Name or Renown: The person who bears "the name" is the first individual God mentions that He will oppose. The Hebrew word for "name" is *shem*. It means name, fame or reputation.[1]

GIANTS IN THE LAND

The first time the Scriptures mention "men of name" refers to those born to rebel angels who mated with Adamite women. "The Nephilim were on the earth in those days, and also afterward, when the sons of God came into the daughters of men, and they bore children to them. Those were the mighty men who were of old, men of renown" (Genesis 6:4). The word "renown" here is the same Hebrew word *shem* used in the Isaiah 14 passage.[2]

Those who bear "the name" are the Nephilim. I believe this name is associated with the fallen angel they come from. If you think about it, the Bible doesn't name these giants, but the Scriptures do describe them as heroes or men of renown. A good reason for this might be so that their names would not be remembered or worshiped.

The Survivors: Next let's discuss who the survivors are that will be destroyed in Babylon. The Hebrew term for "survivors" is *she'ar*, and it means remnant, rest or residue.[3] I believe that the term survivors refer to those born to the giants. They are also considered giants.

Such were the Anakim giants. The Anakim come from the Nephilim according to Numbers 13:33.

Offspring and Posterity: Two other groups who will be cut off at Babylon are the offspring and posterity. The term "offspring" in Hebrew is *niyn*, which means son. "Posterity" in Hebrew is *neked* and means son's son.[4, 5] The Bible uses the two terms only in the context of non-Adamite lineages.

The first time these two terms are mentioned in Scripture is in Genesis when Abraham converses with Abimelech. Let's look at the passage:

> Now it came about at that time that Abimelech and Phichol, the commander of his army, spoke to Abraham, saying, "God is with you in all that you do; now therefore, swear to me here by God that you will not deal falsely with me or with my offspring or with my posterity, but according to the kindness that I have shown to you, you shall show to me and to the land in which you have sojourned." (Genesis 21:22 and 23)

GIANTS IN THE LAND

Abimelech asked Abraham to deal honorably with him, and the next two generations, which were his "offspring," defined in the passage as *niyn* and "posterity" as *neked*.[6, 7] Abraham agreed. But who was King Abimelech? King Abimelech was the king of Gerar, a Philistine town that is possibly the site of modern-day Um Jerrar near the coast southwest of Gaza (Genesis 20:2 - 21:32). In Joshua 13:2 and 3, the passage indicates that the Avvites lived in ancient Philistia. Avvites also were called Avvim. The Avvim were giants. Therefore, we can deduce that King Abimelech was a giant.

The Babylonian Talmud (Hullin 60b) makes this observation:

> In as much as Abimelech adjured Abraham saying, Thou wilt not deal falsely with me, nor with my son, nor with my son's son, the Holy One, blessed be He, said, Let the Kaphtorim come and take away the land from the Avvim, who are Philistines, and then Israel may come and take it away from the Kaphtorim.[8]

(6) Gen. XXI, 23

GIANTS IN THE LAND

The Avvim were the early occupants of Philistia in the days of Abraham, according to the Bible.

To further clarify, when it came time for the Israelites to conquer the land of Canaan – a land infested with giant descendants such as the Amorites, Perizzites, Hivites and Jebusites – the Scriptures record that the Caphtorim, who came from Caphtor, defeated the Avvim (see Deuteronomy 2:23). The Israelites didn't conquer them. The Israelites couldn't remove them from the land of Canaan because Abraham made an agreement with King Abimelech not to harm his offspring (*niyn*) and his posterity (*neked*).[9, 10] Abimelech and his descendants weren't normal human beings that interacted with Abraham.

The other place the two terms, *niyn* and *neked* are mentioned is in Job. Job writes of the wicked:

> His roots are dried below, and his branch is cut off above. Memory of him perishes from the earth, and he has no name abroad. He is driven from light into darkness, and chased from the inhabited world. He has no offspring *[niyn]* or

posterity *[neked]* among his people, nor any survivor where he sojourned. (Job 18:16-19)

Job gives no indication that these individuals were Adamite. In chapter 27 he indicates a wicked man and describes him as an `adam.[11] He states: "This is the portion of a wicked man [this is the word `adam] from God, and the inheritance *which* tyrants receive from the Almighty. Though his sons are many, they are destined for the sword; and his descendants will not be satisfied with bread" (Job 27:13 and 14). If the "wicked" were Adamites in Job 18:16-19, then Job would have said so.

These who will be the offspring and posterity of a giant will also meet their doom in Babylon. Punishment will occur after several generations with this giant and its descendants. And what a punishment it will be! The Lord will annihilate them.

Judgment of giants and their descendants

God's judgment takes place with giants and their descendants after several generations. I cannot give you the exact generation when these polluted beings are cut off. That's because Isaiah's prophecy describes classes of pollution more so than a specific number of generations.

The Bible emphasizes a similar judgment occurred in the past with giants and their descendants. Let's trace one giant tribe and their descendants. This will allow us to see the timing of God's judgment that came upon these non-humans. Let's look at the Rephaim who were giants. The Rephaim had offspring. They were called the Amorites. We discussed an earlier chapter how it is that the Amorites were the offspring of the Rephaim. The Amorites also had offspring. They were called the Gibeonites. Second Samuel 21:2 reveals this. "So the king called the Gibeonites and spoke to them (now the Gibeonites were not of the sons of Israel but of the remnant of the Amorites, and the sons of Israel made a covenant with them, but Saul had sought to kill them in his zeal for the sons of Israel and Judah)."

When it came time to conquer Canaan, the Israelites fought against Og, one of the last Rephaim, and many Amorites on their way to Canaan and defeated them. They defeated additional Amorites while in Canaan.

But the Gibeonites whom they were told to dispossess deceived them into making a covenant with them and therefore, they were not allowed to remove them from the land (Joshua 9).

We've observed what appear to have been a few generations of giant pollution: Rephaim, Amorites and Gibeonites. But there was more. Many generations of Amorites existed during the time the Israelites dwelt in Egypt which was before they went to possess the land of Canaan. This lets us know that several generations of giant pollution existed before the time they were dealt with by God.

We've only tracked one giant tribe and their descendants and how they were dealt with. But there were other giant tribes and their descendants who occupied the land of Canaan. The Israelites battled and defeated many of them.

God caused the Israelites to obtain victory in their conquest of Canaan. I believe one of the reasons why Israel experienced victory was because it was time for God to judge these polluted beings. Like in times past,

God will judge future giants and their descendants after several generations.

The Bible doesn't name future giants. But it doesn't mean they won't appear. At times, God speaks in symbols, patterns, and parables so that the inquisitive may dig deeper into His Word. Giants appear in future events described in the Scriptures, but in a different way. It's as if God hid them to reveal them. Now it's time for us – believers – to know about them. Had we recognized the presence of future giants sooner, I believe fear would have struck our hearts about the future.

Some information I discovered in my research about giants emerged from the genealogies. Truths about these hybrid beings inundate the long lists of names that once made me sleepy when reading them. I'm reminded of the verse that says: "All Scripture is inspired by God and profitable for teaching, for reproof, for correction, for training in righteousness" (2 Timothy 3:16).

We can conclude that a giant and several

generations of its descendants will exist before the Second Coming of Christ, and Babylon is where they will live. I believe we need to consider how soon we think we will see the physical manifestation of giants in the land.

GIANTS IN THE LAND

CHAPTER 5
GIANT INFILTRATION

Giants infiltrated society before and after the flood as depicted in Genesis. They were visible and vicious figures that we can read about in the Bible and history.

Before the flood

Giants were on the earth during the antediluvian age. The Bible records: "God looked on the earth, and behold, it was corrupt; for all flesh had corrupted their way upon the earth. Then God said to Noah, 'The end of all flesh has come before me, for the earth is filled with violence because of them; and behold, I am about to destroy them with the earth' " (Genesis 6:12 and 13). That He did. A catastrophic flood wiped out every living thing on the face of the earth except for those who boarded an ark to escape.

Noah and his family were the human survivors who escaped the deluge. The Bible says, "Noah was a righteous man, blameless in his time; Noah walked with God" (Genesis 6:9b). *Tamiym* is the Hebrew term for "blameless."[1] It means he was without blemish; he was pure adamic stock. He wasn't contaminated by giants. By choosing to rescue Noah from the flood, it appears as if God sought to preserve the *human* race.

Some people think all that were swept away in the flood were giants or those contaminated by them. However, this is not the case. The Bible says regarding the flood in Genesis 6:7, "The Lord said, 'I will blot out man whom I have created from the face of the land, from man to animals to creeping things and to birds of the sky; for I am sorry that I have made them.' "

"Man" in this passage is the Hebrew term *'adam*.[2] Giants, and their descendants, are never described as

Adamites in the Scriptures. This tells us that there were Adamites among those swept away in the flood.

Some may think God acted cruelly by wiping out most of mankind. A good point to make is that Noah was a preacher of righteousness. He must have preached to those around him to get right with God. Clearly, they didn't listen. Only a few Adamites boarded the ark, but God's desire all along was for every Adamite to live sheltered from the storm. Oh! The love of God!

I believe it will be just like Noah's time at the end of the age. People will be unwilling to turn from evil doing. The Book of Revelation says that even the holy angels will preach the gospel. God desires for all of mankind to turn to Jesus with their whole heart.

After the flood

Giant infestations reappeared after the flood. Noah's lineage - through whom God repopulated the earth – featured this spiritual rottenness.

Shem, a son of Noah, from his line come the

Israelites. Some of the Israelites mingled with the giant-polluted inhabitants of the land of Canaan according to Judges 3:6.

Ham, another son of Noah, one of his sons mingled with giants (Genesis 10:15-18 and 27:46). The name of Ham's son who mixed with giants was Canaan. From Canaan's line came the Amorites, Girgashites, Hivites and some others.

Many have taught that Canaan's line was the only line polluted by giants because he incurred a curse. But Canaan was cursed before he got involved with giants. The Bible records that after the flood, Noah became drunk in his tent and became uncovered. "Ham, the father of Canaan, saw the nakedness of his father, and told his two brothers outside" (Genesis 9:22). Canaan, the son of Ham, was cursed by Noah because of it: "Cursed be Canaan; a servant of servants he shall be to his brothers" (Genesis 9:25b). The sin is unclear. However, the curse says that Canaan and his descendants would be the lowliest servants. Some believe that Canaan's curse meant giants would infiltrate his line. But the Scriptures express it differently.

Upon close examination giants infiltrated the line of Noah. There are other Biblical accounts of giant infiltration. I've only named a few.

GIANTS IN THE LAND

CHAPTER 6
WHAT WILL GIANT POLLUTION LOOK LIKE?

Giants will appear on the earth again. For this reason, we need to understand how the Bible depicts a polluted family line. When we understand that, we can identify and prepare to confront the spiritual chaos that lies ahead.

Giant pollution starts when angels leave their proper domain and have relations with human women. Children born from these unions are considered giants. Because technology is advancing rapidly, I don't know whether angels will have physical relations with women. What I do know is that in whatever way rebellious angels initiate unholy unions, earthborn giants will be the result. The appearance of these non-Adamites will have widespread consequences.

Polluted women and the children who descend from them

It's understood that male giants who have relations with human women can pollute their children. But what about female giants, can they infect a bloodline? The Bible has something to say about this pollution as well.

I have discovered that if a highly giant-polluted female mixes with a human male, children born to her assume her bloodline, and not that of their human father. Normally, human children assume the bloodline of their fathers. Here's a case in point. Buried within the genealogy of Esau is the bloodline of a female that carries a strong giant pollution who had relations with Esau. The Bible records that Esau married Adah, Aholibamah, and Basemath. Let's look at the nature these three women possessed.

Esau's wife, Adah, father was a Hittite. Hittites were giant descendants.

Basemath was a daughter of Ishmael, who was Abraham's son through Hagar the Egyptian. The Bible offers us clues Basemath's family lineage was once contaminated by giants. Basemath was also called Mahalath, which means stringed instrument.[1] The root of this word goes back to *chalah*, which means sickness or diseased.[2] Basemath's brother was Nebajoth, which means height.[3] Basemath's name and that of her brother's indicate her family lineage was once giant-infected. (Genesis 21:21 and 28:9).

Aholibamah was a daughter of a Horite and granddaughter of a Hivite. Both tribes were giant descendants.

Esau had children by these women. The question is, were any of these women infected by giants and did any pollute their children?

Let's go back to Esau's wife, Aholibamah. Her name means "tent of the high place."[4] To me, this implies some form of idolatry or ritual activity. Aholibamah was a striking female who was highly giant-polluted. Again, she was the daughter of a Horite and granddaughter of a Hivite. The Bible traces her descendants back to her, and not Esau. Genesis 36:18 (NKJV) reads: "And these were the sons of Aholibamah, Esau's wife: Chief Jeush, Chief Jaalam, and Chief Korah. These were the chiefs who descended from Aholibamah, Esau's wife, the daughter of Anah." This was my first indication that Esau's genealogy was abnormal.

Greek mythology and contemporary films depict images of tall, muscular female warriors. So does the Bible. According to these passages, tall and powerful women existed.

The Bible says Esau grieved his parents by marrying women from Canaan. I can see why Esau's marital choices troubled Isaac and Rebecca. Esau's wives came from giant-polluted lineages and one was still infected by giants somehow (Genesis 26:35b and 36:1-3).

Esau's marriages were disastrous. Some of his

children were giant-polluted. His descendants intensely hated the Israelites, and God eventually brought punishment upon Edom (Esau) for their hateful activities against the Israelites (Jeremiah 49:7-22).

Here's my point. Since a highly giant-polluted female who had relations with a human male polluted their children, then so can a giant female who does the same thing.

Considering many giants will walk the earth again as they did in times past, it's important to know what is a contaminated bloodline. Because of today's growing religious tolerance, it wouldn't surprise me if Satan tries to deceive people into believing it's OK to mix with giants when these polluted beings appear. If people fall for Satan's lie, their acceptance will strengthen the next generation of pollution. Believers must resist this kind of thinking. We must never forget that God opposes giant pollution. He forbids our participation in this deception.

God opposes humans mixing with giants

God commanded the Israelites not to mingle with

the giant-polluted inhabitants of Canaan because their children would become contaminated. At times, God required disobedient Israelites to move away from their brethren because they disobeyed His instructions to separate from the inhabitants of Canaan. God set boundaries between Israel and giants and giant descendants because these populations inevitably turned the Israelites away from Him, the Most High God. Deluded by their idolatry, those disobedient Israelites sometimes named their children after the inhabitants of the land idols and abandoned the God of their fathers Abraham, Isaac, and Jacob. What a shame!

When Israelites mingled with giants or their descendants, they experienced torment and captivity. The Bible records this in Judges 3:

> The sons of Israel lived among the Canaanites, the Hittites, the Amorites, the Perizzites, the Hivites, and the Jebusites; and they took their daughters for themselves as wives, and gave their daughters to their sons, and served their gods. The sons of Israel did what was evil in the sight of the LORD, and forgot the LORD their

God and served the Baals and Asheroth. Then the anger of the LORD was kindled against Israel, so that He sold them into the hands of Cushan-rishathaim king of Mesopotamia; and the sons of Israel served Cushan-rishathaim eight years. (Judges 3:5-8)

The giant-polluted inhabitants of Canaan worshiped the Baals, who were male gods, and the Asheroth, who were the female counterparts. God never wanted the Israelites to intermingle with these populations. He wanted a holy seed, a people set apart for Himself. He still does.

GIANTS IN THE LAND

CHAPTER 7
GIANTS ARE NOT REDEEMED

When giants reappear on the earth, they'll resemble human beings, but they'll also look different. They'll be able to contaminate a human bloodline as they did in biblical times. But there is another critical distinction to make. Giants or their polluted descendants won't possess the same spiritual capacity as human beings. In other words, they aren't eligible to be redeemed by the blood of Christ. They can't benefit from the work of Jesus. I discovered this fact by noting that every time the Bible introduces giants or their descendants, the Scriptures never refer to them as Adamites or human beings.

Jesus came to save you and me. Not giants or their descendants. The Book of Hebrews conveys this truth:

> Forasmuch then as the children are partakers of flesh and blood, he also himself likewise took part of the same; that through death he might destroy him that had the power of death, that is, the devil; and deliver them who through fear of death were all their lifetime subject to bondage. For verily he took not on him the nature of angels; but he took on him the seed of Abraham. Wherefore in all things it behoved him to be made like unto his brethren, that he might be a merciful and faithful high priest in things pertaining to God, to make reconciliation for the sins of the people. (Hebrews 2:14-17 KJV)

The seed of Abraham refers to Adamites. When Jesus Christ took on the identity of a human being, he reconciled Adamites to God. Giants and their offspring aren't like normal mankind and don't experience the opportunity for redemption like normal people. I present this point here because we must keep in mind what the Bible says regarding their fate. Remember, God didn't authorize angels to have relations with human women, so giants don't exist by God's plan but by the activities of rebellious angels and, ultimately, Satan.

The redemption of human beings

When I first started teaching on the subject of giants, someone asked, "What does this have to do with our redemption?" The future appearance of giants has everything to do with the gift of salvation for humans. God wants to bring many *human* sons and daughters to glory. By faith in Jesus Christ, and by accepting what He accomplished on the cross, we are translated from the kingdom of darkness and into the kingdom of God. If a family line becomes spiritually polluted by giants, then those infected descendants can't receive salvation because *they are not* human.

GIANTS IN THE LAND

CHAPTER 8
GOD WANTS TO PRESERVE LIFE

The central theme throughout the Old Testament was for Abraham and his descendants to fulfill God's mission. The Lord charged Abraham and his descendants to enter the Promised Land and dispossess the inhabitants, an abominable group of non-Adamites. During the time of Jacob, the grandson of Abraham, his descendants moved from Canaan because of a famine and lived in Egypt. They became slaves and lived there for over 400 years.

GIANTS IN THE LAND

While trapped in slavery, Jacob's descendants, known as Israelites, cried out to God because of Egyptian oppression. In response, God released them from the iron grip of Egypt and led them back to – guess where – the land of Canaan. God's mission, first given to Abraham, had not changed. God told the Israelites on their way to possessing Canaan: "I will deliver the inhabitants of the land into your hand, and you will drive them out before you" (Exodus 23:31a).

The inhabitants of Canaan were mostly giants and giant descendants. The land was polluted. When the Israelites entered Canaan after leaving Egypt, God instructed them to drive out the inhabitants. Over the course of time, the Israelites drove out most of them. The remaining giant descendants troubled Israel immensely (Numbers 33:55).

The Old Testament recounts many battles between the Israelites and giant descendants of Canaan. The Israelites fought other battles, and other events occurred during their lives, but the hostilities between the Israelites and the inhabitants of Canaan represented the battle of battles. God relentlessly thwarted Satan's attempts to defile the Israelites irrevocably with giants and their descendants. He also destroyed Satan's efforts to prevent the seed of the coming Messiah from emerging from the line of Judah, one of the twelve tribes of Israel.

God used many of His people to rid the land of giants and their descendants, including King David. God loved David and affirmed his kingship because he courageously performed the God-given mission to destroy giants descendants in the regions God instructed David to conquer. Even modern-day Israel faces conflicts in those regions. Let me emphasize that I'm not saying the family lines of people in those regions are giant-infected today. It's clear, however, that spiritual darkness in those regions continues to persist within the conflict.

It's also apparent from ancient artifacts and histories that giants reached other parts of the world. The biblical narrative focuses on the Israelites' story, but I believe that God also had other people groups destroy these giants and their descendants.

New school of thought

Many Bible students ask the question: "Why did God allow women and children to be wiped out during some of Israel's battles while en route and in the land of Canaan?" First of all, we first must understand that God is good in all His ways. Cruelty was not the reason God dispossessed the inhabitants of Canaan. He charged Israel with overthrowing them because the giants' wickedness was abominable and a pernicious influence on mankind. Canaan's inhabitants who were giants and giant descendants were polluted, violent, and beyond redemption. God judged them so that they would not destroy the Adamite race (Deuteronomy 3:16).

Once I understood this, God's kindness overwhelmed me even more. He loves human beings passionately! He has preserved the life of mankind throughout history. Because we frequently don't understand His ways, God's judgments may appear unjust when they are deeply compassionate. God is a gracious Father, and He protects His children from irreversible harm.

CHAPTER 9
ACTIVITIES OF FUTURE GIANTS

Now that we understand giants will appear on the earth again, but what will they do? Once more we must turn to the Bible for an accurate depiction of how giants and their descendants will live among us and radically change the world.

Giants influenced others toward idolatry

Giants were known for turning people's hearts away from God to the worship of idols. Giants worshiped rebellious angels as gods. Giant descendants believed their giant parents – those of angelic and human descent – were demigods. Many times they offered their children by death to them.

Some of the Israelites were influenced by these polluted beings and took up this awful activity of idolatry. Psalm 106:35-41 reveals:

> But they mingled with the nations and served their idols which became a snare to them. They even sacrificed their sons and their daughters to the demons. And shed innocent blood. The blood of their sons and daughters, whom they sacrificed to the idols of Canaan. And the land was polluted with the blood. Thus they became unclean in their practices, and played the harlot in their deeds. Therefore the anger of the LORD was kindled against His people and He abhorred His inheritance. Then He gave them into the hand of the nations, and those who hated them ruler over them.

God instructed the Israelites not to repeat the actions of Canaan's giant-polluted inhabitants when they occupied the land (Exodus 23:24). Unfortunately some did. Those Israelites who co-mingled with giants or their descendants hearts turned from God to the worship of idols. In the future we must watch for giants who will want to allure some of mankind away from serving God.

Giants practiced immoral relations

Giant beings practiced immoral relations. And so did their descendants.

God cautioned the Israelites not to conduct their relations as the polluted beings did in the land of Canaan when they went to possess the land. Leviticus 18 records their practices. Because the passage is quite lengthy I provided you with a condense list of their practices instead of quoting the passage. Giant populations practiced incest, relations with close relatives, polygamy, adultery, homosexuality, lesbianism and bestiality according to Leviticus 18.

God cautioned the Israelites to not do the same practices. "For the men of the land who have been before you have done all these abominations, and the land has become defiled; so that the land might not spew you out, should you defile it, as it has spewed out the nation which had been before you." (Leviticus 18:27 and 28) By the way, "men" in the passage is the Hebrew term `iysh which means male.[1] It's not the term `adam which refers to humankind.[2]

When giants appear in the future, we can expect them to perform the same immoral relations as those giant-populations did in the past.

Giants practiced witchcraft

Giants were into the supernatural but not in a good way. They practiced witchcraft. I use this term in a broad sense. Deuteronomy 18:10 – 14 reveals:

> There shall not be found among you anyone who makes his son or his daughter pass through the fire, who uses divination, one who practices witchcraft, or one who interprets omens, or a sorcerer, or one who casts a spell, or a medium, or a spiritist, or one who calls up the dead. For whoever does these things is detestable to the LORD; and because of these detestable things

the LORD your God will drive out them before you. You shall be blameless before the LORD your God. For those nations, which you shall dispossess, listen to those who practice witchcraft and to diviners, but as for you, the LORD your God has not allowed you *to do* so."

The practice of witchcraft is strictly forbidden by God. This practice can open the door to demonic activity in one's life. Giants who will appear will practice witchcraft.

Giants changed moral laws

An ancient Babylonian monarch established one of the earliest set of laws. He is a picture of how giants and their descendants attempt to alter God's moral standard.

History recounts that King Hammurabi was the "sixth and best-known ruler of the first (Amorite) dynasty of Babylon (reigning *c.* 1792-50 BC). Noted for his surviving set of laws, his code once was considered the oldest promulgation of laws in human history. Hammurabi had a tribal Amorite name."[3] More than likely he was a descendant of an Amorite.

Archaeologists discovered "The Code of Hammurabi" in 1901. The code features an etched picture of Hammurabi communicating with a false god and lists various laws. The king states that gods called him to rule in the land.[4]

The laws include civil, criminal, and family matters. The layout clearly outlines its punishments should one break the law. In some places, the laws sound reasonable, in others places they do not mirror the fruit of the Spirit of God. But that is Satan's familiar tactic: Mix the good with the bad. In the future, giants will seek to change moral laws.

Giants performed violent acts

The Old Testament describes how Og, a giant king, and those of his kingdom attacked the Israelites who were en route to Canaan. They wouldn't allow the Israelites to pass peacefully through their land (Deuteronomy 3 and Joshua 12). Og and those of his kingdom had no reason for antagonizing human beings but did so out of malice.

GIANTS IN THE LAND

A son of a Hivite raped Dinah, the only daughter of the patriarch Jacob (Genesis 34:1 and 2). He preyed on her when she went out to see the daughters of the land in Canaan. The Hivites were descendants of a giant. Future giants and their descendants will commit violent acts.

Giants and their descendants will live among us and radically change the world by influencing others toward idolatry, practicing witchcraft, changing laws, performing violent acts and tempting people to perform immoral relations.

GIANTS IN THE LAND

CHAPTER 10
WHAT CAN WE EXPECT?

As Bible students, we often quote Jesus as saying that a sign of His return will be the era's resemblance to the days of Noah and Lot. Have we fully understood Jesus' words? Let's review them again:

> And as it was in the days of Noah, so it will be also in the days of the Son of Man: They ate, they drank, they married wives, they were given in marriage, until the day that Noah entered the ark and the flood came and destroyed them all. Likewise as it was also in the days of Lot: They

ate, they drank, they bought, they sold, they planted, they built; but on the day that Lot went out of Sodom it rained fire and brimstone from heaven and destroyed them all. Even so will it be in the day when the Son of Man is revealed. (Luke 17:26-30)

We often interpret this passage only to mean that everyday life will continue like usual at the Second Coming of Christ, but Jesus includes a significant description. He says this period will resemble the days of Noah and Lot. A careful study of the historical surroundings of these men reveals that giants existed.

As absurd as it may seem, many giants will populate the earth again along with their descendants before the end of this age – just as they did during the times of Noah and Lot. Jesus' words will come true.

Conclusion

We live in a season when God is accelerating our understanding about giants to prepare us for their future reappearance. But you may wonder why God is allowing giants to appear on the earth again. I believe the Bible teaches that giants are coming to fulfill His wrath. He will use them to destroy Babylon, for example, as we saw earlier in Isaiah chapters 13 and 14. Proverbs 16:4 also underscores the point that God is in total control: "The LORD has made everything for its own purpose, even the wicked for the day of evil."

Knowledge about giants and their descendants must not lead us to hasty actions or judgments. Understanding their origins and behaviors should create within us a richer dependence on God for wisdom.

According to the Scriptures, when God dealt with giants and their descendants in ancient history, He moved judiciously and within His appointed time. We can trust Him to do so again! We must remember that the corrupt nature of giants will lead to their own ruin.

The global impact of giants and their descendants during these last days will be huge. I'm not sharing this information to incite eschatological hype or fear. My intent is to heighten awareness about things to come. Hopefully, this book will inspire believers to pray fervently because we will once again see giants in the land.

God bless you.

GLOSSARY

These terms aided my research and navigation on the subject of giants. You may find them helpful too.

Adam – This Hebrew word means red. Adam was the husband of Eve (Strong's number 121).

`adam – This Hebrew word means man or mankind (Strong's number 120).

Adamites – Human beings who descend from Adam and Eve. That's people like you and me.

Day of the Lord – A period also known as the "Day of the Lord's Wrath." At this time, the Lamb of God (Jesus Christ) and God Himself will pour out great fury because of iniquity and evil done upon the earth.

End of the age – A period on the earth when human history as we know it concludes. The time of Noah when the great flood occurred was a different age from ours. Jesus returns to earth close to the end of the age.

The era after the end of the age is considered the thousand-year reign of Christ, which takes place on the earth.

giants – Non-Adamite beings who descends from an angelic being and human being.

giant descendants – Non-Adamite beings who are of the line of a giant.

giant offspring – Non-Adamite beings on earth who are born to giants.

gibbowr – The Hebrew word often taken to mean strong. The plural word is *gibborim*.

'iysh – The Hebrew word for male or husband.

Millennium Reign of Christ – This is a time when Christ will reign on earth for a thousand years. It will be a time of peace.

Nephilim – These are non-Adamite beings born on earth. They are the offspring of rebellious angels and Adamite women.

Satan – This word means adversary or enemy. Satan is also called the devil.

Second Coming of Christ – A term referring to the return of the Lord Jesus Christ to the earth.

Sons of God – This phrase refers to a class of angels in the Old Testament. In the New Testament, believers are called sons of God.

ENDNOTES

CHAPTER 1

1. Brown, Driver, Briggs and Gesenius. "Hebrew Lexicon entry for 'adam". "The Old Testament Hebrew Lexicon". http://www.studylight.org/lex/heb/view.cgi?number=120.

2. Brown, Driver, Briggs and Gesenius. "Hebrew Lexicon entry for Naphal". "The Old Testament Hebrew Lexicon". http://www.studylight.org/lex/heb/view.cgi?number=5307.

3. Brown, Driver, Briggs and Gesenius. "Hebrew Lexicon entry for Gibbowr". "The Old Testament Hebrew Lexicon". http://www.studylight.org/lex/heb/view.cgi?number=1368.

CHAPTER 2

1. Easton, Matthew George. "Entry for 'Rephaim, Valley of'". "Easton's Bible Dictionary". http://www.studylight.org/dic/ebd/view.cgi?number=T3108.

2. Easton, Matthew George. "Entry for 'Goliath' ". "Easton's Bible Dictionary". http://www.studylight.org/dic/ebd/view.cgi?number=T1523. Reference cubic

3. Brown, Driver, Briggs and Gesenius. "Hebrew Lexicon entry for `Anaqiy". "The Old Testament Hebrew Lexicon". http://www.studylight.org/lex/heb/view.cgi?number=6062.

4. Brown, Driver, Briggs and Gesenius. "Hebrew Lexicon entry for 'Eymiym". "The Old Testament Hebrew Lexicon". http://www.studylight.org/lex/heb/view.cgi?number=368.

5. Brown, Driver, Briggs and Gesenius. "Hebrew Lexicon entry for Zamzom". "The Old Testament Hebrew Lexicon". http://www.studylight.org/lex/heb/view.cgi?number=2157.

6. Brown, Driver, Briggs and Gesenius. "Hebrew Lexicon entry for `Avviym' ". "The Old Testament Hebrew Lexicon". http://www.studylight.org/lex/heb/view.cgi?number=5761.

7. http://www.jewishencyclopedia.com/articles/1422-amorites

8. Brown, Driver, Briggs and Gesenius. "Hebrew Lexicon entry for 'iysh". "The Old Testament Hebrew Lexicon". http://www.studylight.org/lex/heb/view.cgi?number=376

9. Ibid., Strong's number 120 'adam

10. Ibid., Strong's number 376 'iysh

11. Ibid., Reference Cubic

CHAPTER 3

1. Ibid., Strong's number 1368 Gibbowr

2. Jamieson, Robert, D.D. "Commentary on Isaiah 13". "Commentary Critical and Explanatory on the Whole Bible". http://www.studylight.org/com/jfb/view.cgi?book=isa&chapter=013. 1871.

3. Brown, Driver, Briggs and Gesenius. "Hebrew Lexicon entry for Kacday". "The Old Testament Hebrew Lexicon". Reference Chaldeans http://www.studylight.org/lex/heb/view.cgi?number=3679.

4. U.S. Department of State, Media Note, Office of the Spokesman, Washington, DC, January 7, 2009. http://exchanges.state.gov/heritage/iraq/pdfs/babylonprojmedianote.pdf.

CHAPTER 4

1. Brown, Driver, Briggs and Gesenius. "Hebrew Lexicon entry for Shem". "The Old Testament Hebrew Lexicon". http://www.studylight.org/lex/heb/view.cgi?number=8034.

2. Ibid., Strong's number 8034 shem

3. Brown, Driver, Briggs and Gesenius. "Hebrew Lexicon entry for Sha'ar". "The Old Testament Hebrew Lexicon". http://www.studylight.org/lex/heb/view.cgi?number=7604.

4. Brown, Driver, Briggs and Gesenius. "Hebrew Lexicon entry for Niyn". "The Old Testament Hebrew Lexicon". http://www.studylight.org/lex/heb/view.cgi?number=5209.

5. Brown, Driver, Briggs and Gesenius. "Hebrew Lexicon entry for Neked". "The Old Testament Hebrew Lexicon". http://www.studylight.org/lex/heb/view.cgi?number=5220.

6. Ibid., Strong's number 5209 niyn

7. Ibid., Strong's number 5220 neked

8. Translated into English by Cashdan, Eli. Under the editorship of Epstein, Rabbi Dr. I. Hebrew - English Edition of the Babylonian Talmud: Hullin, Published by The Soncino Press, 1980. Hullin 60b

9. Ibid., Strong's number 5209 niyn

10. Ibid., Strong's number 5220 neked

11. Ibid., Strong's number 120 'adam

CHAPTER 5

1. Brown, Driver, Briggs and Gesenius. "Hebrew Lexicon entry for Tamiym". "The Old Testament Hebrew Lexicon". http://www.studylight.org/lex/heb/view.cgi?number=8549.

2. Ibid., Strong's number 120 'adam

CHAPTER 6

1. Brown, Driver, Briggs and Gesenius. "Hebrew Lexicon entry for Machalath". "The Old Testament Hebrew Lexicon". http://www.studylight.org/lex/heb/view.cgi?number=4258.

2. Brown, Driver, Briggs and Gesenius. "Hebrew Lexicon entry for Chalah". "The Old Testament Hebrew Lexicon". http://www.studylight.org/lex/heb/view.cgi?number=2470.

3. Brown, Driver, Briggs and Gesenius. "Hebrew Lexicon entry for N@bayowth". "The Old Testament Hebrew Lexicon". http://www.studylight.org/lex/heb/view.cgi?number=5032.

4. Brown, Driver, Briggs and Gesenius. "Hebrew Lexicon entry for 'Oholiybamah". "The Old Testament Hebrew Lexicon". http://www.studylight.org/lex/heb/view.cgi?number=173.

CHAPTER 9

1. Ibid., Strong's number 376 'iysh

2. Ibid., Strong's number 120 'adam

3. The Encyclopedia Britannica, 15th Edition. Volume 5, Chicago, Illinois. "Hammurabi." See page 668.

4. Harper, Robert Francis. The Code of Hammurabi, Second Edition, The University of Chicago Press, Chicago, Illinois, 1904. See page 3.

REONA MARTIN MINISTRIES

To contact e-mail: reona@reonamartinministries.com

Website: www.reonamartinministries.com

Notes

Notes

Notes

Notes

Notes

Notes

www.ingramcontent.com/pod-product-compliance
Lightning Source LLC
Chambersburg PA
CBHW070321100426
42743CB00011B/2504